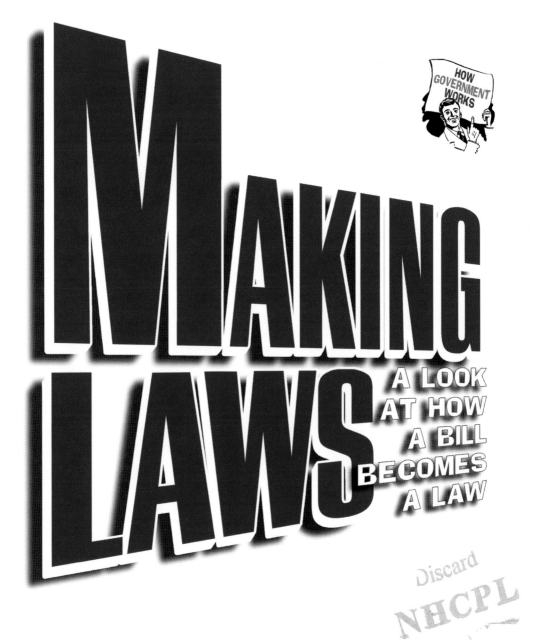

MAKING LAWS

A LOOK AT HOW A BILL BECOMES A LAW

HOW GOVERNMENT WORKS

By Sandy Donovan

↳ LERNER P   INNEAPOLIS

Lerner Publications Company
A division of Lerner Publishing Group
241 First Avenue North
Minneapolis, MN 55401 U.S.A.

Website address: www.lernerbooks.com

Library of Congress Cataloging-in-Publication Data

Donovan, Sandra, 1967–
    Making laws : a look at how a bill becomes a law / by Sandy Donovan.
       v. cm. — (How government works)
    Includes bibliographical references and index.
    Contents: It all starts with an idea: people and interest groups—
Introducing . . . —Getting a fair hearing: the committee stage—Traffic cop: the
rules committee and calendars—On the floor: debating and voting—Sorting
things out: conference committees—To the president: getting signed into law.
    ISBN: 0-8225-1346-3 (lib. bdg. : alk. paper)
    1. Legislation—United States—Juvenile literature. 2. Bill drafting—United
States—Juvenile literature. [1. Legislation. 2. Law.] I. Title. II. Series.
KF4945.Z9D66 2004
328.73'0773—dc21   2002152931

Manufactured in the United States of America
1 2 3 4 5 6 — DP — 09 08 07 06 05 04

TABLE OF CONTENTS

INTRODUCTION: LAWS, LAWS EVERYWHERE

QUICK QUESTION: Have you ever thought about how many different kinds of laws there are in the United States? We have laws that tell us things we can't do (like stealing or driving too fast). We also have laws that tell us things we have to do (like going to school and paying taxes).

Some people think there are too many laws, while other people think there should be more laws. Have you ever heard someone say, "There oughta be a law about that?" Most people generally agree that laws are there for good reasons.

Most laws in the United States are either federal laws or state laws.

(*Above*) Speed limits are one kind of many U.S. laws. This speed-limit sign is in Montana.

State governments make state laws, and they apply only to that state. But federal laws apply to the whole country. The U.S. Congress makes federal laws.

Even though Congress makes federal laws, most state laws are made in a similar way. Citizens, too, can become involved in making laws. Ordinary citizens, even kids, can turn an idea into a law.

President Lyndon B. Johnson signs the Civil Rights Act of 1964 into law. The law began as an idea among citizens.

CHAPTER 1
IT ALL STARTS WITH AN IDEA: PEOPLE AND INTEREST GROUPS

TRUE OR FALSE? Making a new law is complicated. True. A law starts out as an idea in someone's head. People come up with ideas all the time. When people think of an idea for a new law, they might try to get it made into a bill. A bill is an idea for a new law or an idea to change an old law. A senator and a representative bring a bill to Congress.

Suppose, for example, that you and your friends agree that you don't want

(Above) Students meet to research and discuss an idea they think might make a good law.

to go to school on Fridays. Since the law says that kids have to go to school five days a week, you might try to get that law changed. You have already come up with the idea for the new law: no school on Fridays. The next step is to get that idea presented to Congress.

The first thing to do is convince a member of Congress that you have a good idea for a new law. Only congresspeople can make a new law. Not even the president has this power.

CONGRESS

Congress—the House of Representatives (the House) and the Senate—heads the legislative branch of the U.S. government. The legislative branch is in charge of making laws for the whole country. Congress meets in the Capitol Building in Washington, D.C. Congress must approve a bill before it can become a law.

The House of Representatives has 435 members. They are called representatives or congressmen or congresswomen. They serve two-year terms of office. Each state has a certain number of representatives, based on how many people live in the state. California, with its large population, has 45 representatives. Delaware has 1. Each of the fifty states also has two senators, no matter the size of the state. So there are one hundred senators in Congress. Each senator has a six-year term of office.

Members of the 107th Congress are sworn into office. Each senator and representative takes an oath to uphold the Constitution and faithfully carry out the responsibilities of office.

These students are meeting with Senator Hillary Rodham Clinton. When many people support an idea, senators and representatives are more likely to consider it.

One thing that really helps convince a congressperson that you have a good idea for a law is to show this official that a lot of other people agree with you. Voters elect congresspeople to serve them and their states. Both senators and representatives want to know what laws those people want them to make. If a congressperson thinks that a lot of voters don't want to have school on Fridays, then he or she might try to change the law.

When it comes to making laws, senators and representatives care more about what adults think than they do about what children think. This isn't because they don't like kids. It's because kids can't vote, and voters decide who gets elected to Congress. To convince your senator that there should be no school on Fridays, you might first want to convince a group of adults that it's a good idea. Then this group could help convince a member of Congress.

SPECIAL INTEREST GROUPS

In fact, there are special groups that work on convincing senators and representatives that certain ideas should be made into laws. These groups are called interest groups because they focus on one area of interest. The National Education Association (NEA), for instance, focuses on issues that teachers care about. Teachers who belong to the NEA pay a small amount of money to the organization each year.

Students talk about their idea for a law with an interest group. Interest groups show senators and representatives that many people support ideas for new laws.

They can tell the NEA what issues interest them and what laws they want passed. Then the NEA tries to convince congresspeople that the teachers' ideas should be made into law. The interest groups pay people to do this job. These people are called lobbyists. Lobbyists try to convince members of Congress to pass, change, or defeat certain laws.

Interest groups are a big part of how a bill becomes a law. Almost all bills that go to Congress start with interest groups. If you want to get the "no school on Fridays" idea made into a bill, the NEA might be the best place to start. Because the bill focuses on the issue of school, teachers might be interested in it.

LEARN THE LINGO

Lobbyists used to wait in the lobbies, or hallways, outside the House and Senate rooms to talk to senators or representatives. That's how they got their name. In modern times, lobbyists make an appointment and go to the congressperson's office.

Lobbyists wait in a lobby for their meetings with congresspeople.

CHAPTER 2
INTRODUCING . . .

QUICK QUESTION: What if you do get an interest group to lobby for your idea of no school on Fridays? The group's goal is to get the idea introduced in Congress. Introducing an idea makes it an official bill. After a bill has been introduced, Congress can get to work on making it a law.

Only a senator or a representative can introduce a bill in Congress.

(Above) The empty House chamber in the U.S. Capitol Building. When Congress is in session, representatives meet in this room.

In this case, Representative Susan Smith decides to introduce the bill that would cancel school on Fridays. First, she needs to get the bill drafted—get it written in the form of a bill. Staff members write a bill with language that is so precise no one can mistake its meaning.

The senator or representative who introduces a bill is called its sponsor. Representative Smith's name is written at the top of the bill because she is the sponsor. Most bills have many sponsors. This shows that a lot of congresspeople support it. The name of the main sponsor goes first. The next names are called cosponsors or coauthors.

INTRODUCTION

After a bill is drafted, the sponsor introduces it. Each bill has a letter and number code that starts with the initials H.R. These initials stand for House Resolution and show that a bill is from the House of Representatives. The first bill to be introduced in the House during a two-year session, for instance, is called H.R. 1.

Representative Smith's bill—numbered H.R. 1022—isn't introduced out loud. A staff person writes down the bill number in the *Congressional Record*, the daily journal of Congress. Then the Government Printing Office prints the *Congressional Record*. The Speaker of the House decides

Did You KNOW? Anyone can subscribe to the *Congressional Record* or buy individual copies from the Superintendent of Documents, Government Printing Office, Washington, DC, 20402. Bills also are available on microfiche in many libraries and can be found on the Internet.

A bill *(right)* introduced in the House of Representatives during a session of the 41st Congress in 1870. Bills are printed in the *Congressional Record*. The *Record* is published in books *(below)* and online at <http://thomas.loc.gov/home/thomas.html>.

[Printer's No., **444**.

41st CONGRESS.
2D SESSION.

H. R. 850.

IN THE HOUSE OF REPRESENTATIVES

FEBRUARY 4, 1870.

Reported as a substitute to House bill 850, ordered to be printed, and recommitted.

Mr. WHEELER, from the Committee on the Pacific Railroad, reported the following as a substitute to House bill No. 850:

A BILL

Relating to the Western Pacific railroad.

the Western Pacific railroad—the western link in the in of railroads connecting the Atlantic and Pacific Oceans, now completed to Oakland, opposite San Francisco, and is important that the western terminus of said railroad uld be as near as possible to San Francisco, and should have icient accommodations for the travel and commerce passing r said road:

Be it enacted by the Senate and House of Representa- es of the United States of America in Congress assembled, at the island of Yerba Buena, or Goat Island, in the Bay San Francisco, California, is hereby granted to the Western ific Railroad Company, its successors and assigns; *Pro- ed,* That one-third thereof shall be reserved by the United tes, if that amount be found necessary, for fortifica-

what happens to the bill next. The Speaker is the head of the majority party (the party with the most elected representatives) and is the presiding officer (the person in charge) in the House. The Speaker has broad powers and is very important.

Sometimes, when a sponsor introduces a bill in the House, a similar bill is also introduced in the Senate. For a bill to become a law, both the House and the Senate must approve it. Having two bills makes this easier and

Companion bills H.R. 936 and S. 448. Representative George Miller *(above, left)* introduced H.R. 936 in the House. Senator Christopher Dodd *(top, right)* introduced S. 448 in the Senate.

sometimes faster because both houses of Congress are discussing the same topic at about the same time. Similar bills that are introduced in the House and the Senate are called companion bills. Sometimes two companion bills are exactly alike. Other times they are slightly different.

In this case, Representative Smith talks with Senator Joe Moe. She wants him to sponsor a No School on Fridays bill in the Senate. Senator Moe agrees with most of Representative Smith's reasons for her bill, but he thinks there should be a few hours of school on Fridays. Senator Moe coauthors a bill with Senators Jones, Brown, and Mendez. The bill is very similar to Representative Smith's bill, except that it would only cancel school on Friday afternoons.

In the Senate chamber, Senator Moe stands up and introduces his bill. Senate bills have codes that start with S for Senate. Senator Moe introduces his bill by saying, "S. 942, a bill to eliminate school on Friday afternoons. Cosponsored by Senators Jones, Brown, and Mendez." Senator Moe tells the Senate that his bill would cancel school on Friday afternoons.

THE PRESIDENT OF THE SENATE

The vice president serves as the head of the Senate and holds the title "president of the Senate." However, the vice president is not a member of the Senate and rarely appears except on ceremonial occasions or to break a tie vote.

The senators elect a president pro tempore, or a temporary president, to serve as the presiding officer in place of the vice president. This person is usually the senator from the majority party who has served the longest term in the Senate. The president pro tempore, however, assigns this job to another senator each day. That way the senators take turns as presiding officer.

Vice President John Adams was the first president of the Senate, serving from 1789 until 1797.

The majority and minority leaders of the Senate (leaders of the two main political parties), as spokespeople for their political parties, decide to send the bill to the Senate Health, Education, Labor and Pensions Committee. There, committee members will talk about the bill. They will also hear from people who are for and against the bill.

IDEA   SUPPORT   INTEREST GROUP

LOBBY CONGRESSPERSON   BILL INTRODUCED IN THE HOUSE

The No School on Fridays bill started as an idea among students. They presented their idea to the NEA, an interest group, which supported the idea. Together they presented the idea to Representative Smith. She saw that the idea had strong citizen support, so she introduced the idea as a bill in the House.

CHAPTER 3
GETTING A FAIR HEARING: THE COMMITTEE STAGE

QUICK QUESTION: What's next? The Speaker of the House has sent Representative Smith's bill to the House Committee on Education and the Workforce. This group of about fifty House members knows a lot about education and jobs. They will hear arguments from both sides about having no school on Fridays.

(Above) Speaker of the House Dennis Hastert opens the first session of the 108th Congress with the banging of a gavel.

Then they will decide whether the rest of Congress should consider the bill.

Representative Walker, the chairperson of the House Committee on Education and the Workforce, decides if and when the committee will discuss the bill about canceling school on Fridays. She decides that this bill is important, so the committee will discuss it the next day, Tuesday. But instead of having the whole committee discuss the bill, she assigns it to a subcommittee, a smaller group that works on specialized subjects.

LEARN THE LINGO

Both parties in the House of Representatives and the Senate elect a "whip," a person who helps majority and minority leaders work to pass their party's bills.

The House Education Reform Subcommittee is going to discuss Representative Smith's bill. This subcommittee specializes in bills that would change education. They schedule a hearing for 10:00 A.M. on Tuesday. At a hearing, people can tell the subcommittee why they like or dislike the bill. These people include experts on the bill's subject and ordinary people who would be affected if the bill becomes law.

DIG DEEPER

In both the House and in the Senate, the majority leader (called the Speaker in the House of Representatives), the minority leader, and the party whips decide which committee will discuss which bill. This is called referring a bill to committee.

TIME TO DECIDE

At 9:00 A.M. on Tuesday, Representative Smith heads to the hearing room where her bill is going to be discussed. This morning will be very important for her. If she can

Members of a House committee debate a bill in the 1800s. A bill's future rests with committee members. They can decide to pass it or let the bill "die."

CONGRESSIONAL COMMITTEES

Each congressional committee has a special topic, such as education or farming or the military. Senators and representatives become experts on the topics of their committees. House and Senate leaders refer hundreds of bills to these committees. The committees don't even consider most of these bills, however. They table them, or never act on them. This is because committee members don't think the bills have a chance of passing. When this happens, people say a bill "died" in committee.

convince most of the people on the subcommittee that canceling school on Fridays is a good idea, then her bill will have a chance to become a law. But if most of the subcommittee doesn't like the idea, then her bill doesn't stand a chance. Since the representatives on this subcommittee are school experts, the rest of Congress will probably listen to what they think about the bill. At 10:00 A.M., Representative Smith introduces her bill to the subcommittee. She describes how the bill would change the present law and tells why she thinks this is a good idea. She tells the committee that canceling school on Fridays will be good for teachers and kids, and it will save schools lots of money.

"Then they can use this extra money to buy books, or computers, or whatever they need," she says.

Some representatives on the subcommittee don't like this idea. "If kids don't go to school on Fridays, they won't learn enough to go to college," one representative says. Representative Smith tells the member that with the extra books and computers, kids will be able to learn more on Monday through Thursday. Other representatives ask her more questions. She feels nervous, but she is well prepared to answer questions.

Next, a lobbyist from the NEA talks about the bill. "This bill will be good for students because they will have more time for special projects on Fridays," he says. "It will also help teachers because they will have more time to grade papers and prepare lesson plans."

People who are against the bill also talk to the subcommittee. "This is a matter that should be decided by each state, not by the federal government," one of them says.

After many people have talked, the representatives have to decide what to tell the House Committee on Education and the Workforce.

First Lady Laura Bush expresses her support for a bill before the House Education Reform Subcommittee.

Senators work together on bills. They don't always agree on everything and compromise to make progress.

They decide that they like the bill, but they want to make one change. Instead of saying that all schools must close on Fridays, they want to say that schools have the choice of holding classes on Fridays or closing for that day. They want each state to decide for itself. Representative Smith decides that this is a good compromise. It's not exactly the idea she had, but she sees that Congress would probably not vote for her idea. She thinks this is the next best thing.

The House Committee on Education and the Workforce then schedules a "markup" for the bill. The representatives read through the original bill and decide where they need to mark up, or make, changes.

After committee members have finished marking up the bill, they decide whether they should recommend it to the whole House of Representatives. Representative Smith is nervous because she thinks it will be a close vote in the committee. She waits and watches while they vote. All the representatives who are for the bill raise their hands. Of the forty-nine representatives on the committee, only forty-one are present. Representative Smith counts the raised hands at the same time as the committee staff person does. "Nineteen, twenty, twenty-one, twenty-two," she counts. She breathes a sigh of relief. Twenty-two votes is more than half of the members in attendance. Her bill passes.

BILL ASSIGNED TO A
HOUSE COMMITTEE

COMMITTEE VOTE

The No School on Fridays bill, which started as an idea among students, has made its way to Congress. The House and the Senate assigned the bill to committees for review, debate, markup (changes), and vote. Committee members voted to pass the bill out of committee.

Chapter 4
Traffic Cop: The Rules Committee and Calendars

True or False? Representative Smith's bill is on its way to the House. True. Officially, the House Committee on Education and the Workforce has "reported out" the bill. It has come a long way since it was an idea in someone's head. First, a staff person drafted it into a bill. Then, Representative Smith introduced it on the House floor. Senator Moe introduced a companion bill on the Senate floor. Next, a House committee held a hearing on the bill.

> (*Above*) In the same way a police officer directs traffic, the House and Senate calendars and the House Rules Committee direct bills.

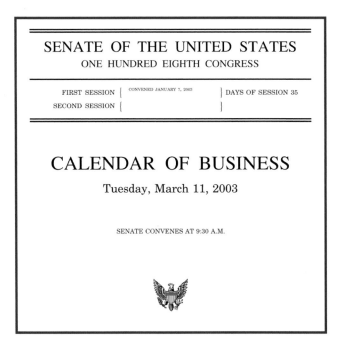

A section from the Senate Calendar of Business. The calendar is updated daily.

People from both sides of the issue talked about the bill. Then the committee voted to recommend it.

MOVING TOWARD THE HOUSE

There is only one more stop before the whole House of Representatives votes on the bill. This stop is a House calendar. This calendar is a list of bills that are waiting to be discussed by either the whole House of Representatives or the whole Senate. The House has four calendars. Bills get assigned to one of them depending on the type of bill. The Senate has only one calendar.

House calendars have many bills on them. Some will never make it to the House floor. The Speaker of the House is in charge of deciding which bills will stay on the calendars.

HOUSE CALENDARS

The House of Representatives has four different calendars, or lists of bills waiting to be discussed by the entire House. Most noncontroversial bills go on the Consent Calendar. This is a list of bills that almost everyone thinks are a good idea, so there is no need for a big discussion about them. Twice a month, the House takes one vote to pass all the bills on the Consent Calendar. The Private Calendar is for private bills that have to do with one person. For instance, one person might need a law that lets him or her become a U.S. citizen. Bills that relate to money, such as raising taxes or paying for the army, go on the Union Calendar. And the Public Calendar is for all public bills that do not deal with money. Most bills are public. For instance, a bill that would make smoking illegal would be a public bill, since everyone would be affected by it. This bill would go on the Public Calendar. The Senate has only one calendar, called the Legislative Calendar.

1. UNION CALENDAR

Rule XIII, clause 1(a):
"(1) A Calendar of the Committee of the Whole House on the state of the Union, to which shall be referred public bills and public resolutions raising revenue, involving a tax or charge on the people, directly or indirectly making appropriations of money or property or requiring such appropriations to be made, authorizing payments out of appropriations already made, releasing any liability to the United States for money or property, or referring a claim to the Court of Claims."

2003			No.
Jan. 28	Referred to the Committee of the Whole House on the State of the Union. (H. Doc. 108–1)	Message of the President of the United States to the Congress on the subject of the state of the Union.	1
H.R. 398 Feb. 13	Mr. Tauzin (Energy and Commerce). Rept. 108–14	To revise and extend the Birth Defects Prevention Act of 1998.	8
H.R. 239 Mar. 5	Mr. Oxley (Financial Services). Rept. 108–22	To facilitate the provision of assistance by the Department of Housing and Urban Development for the cleanup and economic redevelopment of brownfields.	15

The House has four calendars that direct the flow of bills. This picture shows part of the House's Union Calendar from 2003.

THE RULES FOR DEBATING

The House Rules Committee decides on rules for debating bills. There are two main types of rules: open and closed. Open means that representatives will be allowed to amend, or make changes to, bills on the House floor. A closed rule means no changes will be allowed. The Rules Committee can also decide to make no rule about a bill. This means that the bill will sit on a calendar. It will probably never make it to the House floor for a debate and a vote.

But a special committee decides what happens to important bills. This is the House Rules Committee— perhaps the most powerful committee in Congress. The House Rules Committee is powerful because, just like its name says, it makes up the rules for each bill. It decides when bills will be discussed on the House floor. It also decides how long each bill will be debated, or discussed.

The Rules Committee is debating Representative Smith's bill. The members of the committee agree that it is an important bill. They vote to send it to the floor. "We need to allow the entire House to discuss this bill," says Representative Bill Jones, the chairperson of the committee says. They set a date for the bill to come up for debate.

Meanwhile, the Senate Health, Education, Labor and Pensions Committee has approved Senator Moe's bill. The next step for his bill will be discussion by the entire Senate. The Senate does not have a Rules Committee. The majority leader in the Senate is responsible for deciding when bills will be debated on the Senate floor. Current Senate rules don't limit how long senators can debate each bill.

CHAPTER 5
ON THE FLOOR: DEBATING AND VOTING

QUICK QUESTION: What must the House of Representatives do to prepare for a debate on Representative Smith's bill about no school on Fridays? First the representatives vote to make themselves into a committee, called the Committee of the Whole. They do this so they don't have to follow all the strict rules of the full House of Representatives. When the full House votes on something, at least one-half of the representatives (218 of them) must be present.

(Above) Thaddeus Stevens states his opinions about a bill before the Committee of the Whole in 1868. Debates on the House floor can become very passionate.

But when members of the House act as a Committee of the Whole, only 100 representatives need to be present.

On this day, only 110 representatives are present in the House chamber. This is only one-quarter of all the members of the House, but the situation is not unusual. Most House members have already made up their minds about how they are going to vote on Representative Smith's bill. Some representatives are back in their offices getting other work done. Others are at meetings. But the 110 representatives who are present in the House chamber want to debate the bill.

"Who's taking my order—the committee of the whole, or is there a liaison for decaf?"

This political cartoon is poking fun at the long process of getting even the simplest things done through the Committee of the Whole.

An official reading of a bill before the U.S. House of Representatives in 1941

The bill has its second reading. This means it is read to all the members present so they can suggest amendments. The chairperson, usually appointed by the Speaker of the House when the House meets as the Committee of the Whole, lets members talk about an amendment for only five minutes at a time. Total debate time is limited to two hours. The time is divided between the representatives in favor of the bill and those against it. Each side gets one hour.

A representative raises his hand. The chairperson calls on him by saying, "The representative from Maryland." The representative replies, "Thank you, Mr. Chair." Then he suggests a change to the bill. He wants to make sure that if schools save any money by closing on Fridays, they will spend it on computers.

Did You KNOW? Each bill has three official readings. The first reading introduces the bill. The second reading comes before it is debated on the floor. (This is the only time the entire bill is read out loud.) The third reading occurs when the bill is up for a vote.

He reads his amendment. A clerk passes out copies of the amendment.

A few minutes later, the members vote on the amendment to make schools spend the money on computers. All those in favor say "yea." All those against say "nay." This is called a voice vote. Everybody can hear that there are more nays than yeas. The amendment does not pass.

TIME FOR A HOUSE VOTE

Members discuss other amendments, and then the Committee as a Whole has finished its business. It's time to vote on the bill. To vote on any bill, one-half of all the representatives—called a quorum—must be present. A quorum call, which is like a roll call, takes place to see how many members are present. A clerk sets off buzzers in the hallways and offices. This sound tells members that it is time to vote, and they should get to the chamber. All the members hurry to their seats and press a button to be counted. With 240 buttons pressed (more than half of the 435 representatives), a quorum is present.

RIDERS

Some people might like to add amendments that have nothing to do with having school on Fridays. For instance, someone might like to add an amendment that says every school should have a football team. An amendment like this is called a rider. That means that it doesn't have anything to do with the bill. Someone just wants it to "ride" through if the bill becomes a law. But riders are not allowed in the House. All amendments in the House have to have something to do with the bill being debated. In the Senate, however, there are no such rules. Amendments can be about anything. This means that there are often riders on bills that pass the Senate.

This painting shows a voice vote in the House of Representatives in 1868. The voice vote is still used in the House along with electronic voting.

The bill has its third reading, and it is time for the vote. The representatives call out "yea" or "nay." But it is hard to tell if there are more yeas or nays. To make sure, a standing vote is taken. This means all the representatives stand to be counted. One hundred and thirty stand in favor of Representative Smith's bill.

This is enough for the bill to pass, and Representative Smith smiles and shakes hands with the members sitting closest to her. She's happy her bill has passed the House, but more work lies ahead before it becomes a law.

TIME FOR A SENATE VOTE

Exactly one week later, Senator Moe's companion bill comes up for a vote in the Senate. Representative Smith knows that if this bill does not pass the Senate, then her bill will not become a law. She waits anxiously to find out how the Senate will vote.

In the Senate chamber, debating is a little different than it is in the House. For instance, senators do not have a limit on how long they can talk during a debate.

A Senate debate in 1940. This is a rare picture because photography is usually forbidden in the House and Senate chambers.

THE FILIBUSTER

A filibuster is a lot of talking by a senator to prevent a vote on a bill he or she doesn't want to pass. The talking can be about anything. Sometimes senators give long speeches or read books out loud. A filibuster may sound silly, but it is a powerful tool. While a senator is talking, a vote cannot be taken. A filibuster can delay a vote indefinitely. Senators use it when they are against a bill but know that there are not enough votes to defeat it. The only way to end a filibuster is for three-fifths of the full Senate to vote for cloture (an end to the debate). If the vote for cloture passes, a vote must occur within thirty hours. Sometimes just the threat of a filibuster gets other senators to compromise.

(Above) Senator Everett M. Dirksen with papers he read during a long filibuster in 1965

In fact, sometimes senators talk for hours—and even days—at a time, just to delay a vote. These long talking sessions are called filibusters.

Luckily, no one decides to start a filibuster during the debate about no school on Fridays. Senator Moe tells the other senators why he thinks his bill is a good idea. He tells them that his bill would cancel school on Friday afternoons. He also tells them that the bill passed by the House is a little different.

DIG
DEEPER Senators and representatives try to consider as many sides of an issue as they can. Before a bill comes up for debate, they often have their staff prepare short reports on the pros and cons of a bill.

"Under that bill, schools across the country would have different schedules," he says. "But under my bill, all schools would be closed on Friday afternoons. Students could use the time for study and other activities, and teachers could use it to grade papers and prepare for their next classes."

Another senator does not like the bill. "Children need to go to school five days every week. It's the only way they will learn enough!" Even though this senator gets very upset when he disagrees with Senator Moe, he is always polite. He calls Senator Moe "the distinguished senator from California."

It's time to vote on the bill. Senator Moe thinks he has enough votes for his bill to pass. The clerk calls out the senators' names. Most of the senators answer "yea" or "nay." But two say "present." They say this because they do not want to vote either way on the bill. When the clerk has called out all the names, the vote is counted: forty-seven yeas, forty-two nays, and two presents. The bill has passed the Senate.

CHAPTER 6
SORTING THINGS OUT: CONFERENCE COMMITTEES

TRUE OR FALSE? The House and the Senate have voted that schools can close on Fridays, so the bill is a sure thing. False. There's one problem: the bill approved in the House is different from the one approved in the Senate. Senators voted to cancel school on Friday afternoons. But in the House, representatives voted that schools should be able to make their

(Above) Representative Bernie Sanders of Vermont in deep thought. Sometimes getting bills passed is frustrating work.

own decision about having classes on Fridays. Which bill should become a law?

For a bill to become a law, it has to be passed by both the House and the Senate, and the president has to sign it. But in this case, the House and the Senate did not pass the same bill. What can be done?

TIME FOR A CONFERENCE

Conference committees are the way Congress solves this problem. A conference committee is a meeting of both senators and representatives to form a single bill from two similar bills.

The Speaker of the House has assigned seven representatives to be on the conference committee for the No School on Fridays bill. The Senate has assigned seven senators. The fourteen members are meeting at 9:00 A.M.

The meeting room is filled with the fourteen members of the conference committee plus many staff members. The debate gets heated because the senators and representatives all care so much about what happens to the bill. Each side wants its version of the bill to be the final version.

The House members say that kids will never learn anything if the Senate bill is adopted. "We can't tell schools across the whole country that they can't have classes on Friday," says one representative.

Do This!
Find links to House and Senate committee websites as well as links to committee hearing schedules at <http://www.c-span.org>.

This cartoon criticizes a member of Congress for pushing a "pet" (or, favorite) bill through committee, while another is left behind. Sometimes congresspeople favor certain bills over others.

"Some kids need to go to school five full days a week. Some kids even want to go to school five days a week. People in my district would not like this law."

After more discussion, the conference committee gets close to an agreement. The members from the House have convinced the senators that canceling school altogether on Fridays may not be a good idea. The committee members agree that there's a better chance the president would sign the House bill than the Senate bill. After all, the House bill gives states the choice to close school on Fridays. The Senate bill would make all schools close on Friday afternoons.

Next, the committee members prepare a conference committee report. It describes the compromise they reached and tells what the final version of the bill is. Then they send the report to the Senate and the House. Both chambers have to approve the report, just as they voted to approve the earlier versions of the bill.

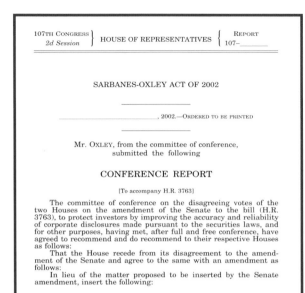

107TH CONGRESS
2d Session } HOUSE OF REPRESENTATIVES { REPORT
107–_____

SARBANES-OXLEY ACT OF 2002

_____, 2002.—ORDERED TO BE PRINTED

Mr. OXLEY, from the committee of conference,
submitted the following

CONFERENCE REPORT

[To accompany H.R. 3763]

The committee of conference on the disagreeing votes of the two Houses on the amendment of the Senate to the bill (H.R. 3763), to protect investors by improving the accuracy and reliability of corporate disclosures made pursuant to the securities laws, and for other purposes, having met, after full and free conference, have agreed to recommend and do recommend to their respective Houses as follows:

That the House recede from its disagreement to the amendment of the Senate and agree to the same with an amendment as follows:

In lieu of the matter proposed to be inserted by the Senate amendment, insert the following:

The title page from a conference committee report

Since the bill in the conference committee report is the same as the House version of the bill, it is easy to get it approved in the House. The report is put on the public calendar, and the speaker schedules a voice vote. When the vote comes up, 342 representatives are present in the chamber. This is enough for a quorum. More than 300 of the members present vote to approve the bill. This is many more than voted to approve it the first time.

In the Senate, it is harder to get the conference committee report approved. When the bill comes up for a vote on the Senate floor, the conference committee members explain why they compromised. "It is better to pass a bill that we know the president will sign than to pass one that has little chance of being signed," says Senator Moe.

When Senator Moe has finished explaining the conference committee report, a vote is called. There are eighty-six senators present. The voice vote is too close to call, so there is a standing vote. First, the senators who are for the bill stand up to be counted. Forty-four senators stand. This is barely enough for the bill to pass. But it is enough, and that is all that matters. Both the House and the Senate have approved the bill. It is time for the final step.

ON TO THE PRESIDENT

The president's desk is the final stop for a bill. After the House and the Senate have approved identical versions of a bill, the bill is printed on official paper. The Speaker of the House and the vice president sign this official document. Then the bill is sent to the president to be signed or vetoed.

TURNING **POINT** When a conference committee agrees on a bill, the bill gets a new name. If the committee adopts the Senate bill, the final name will start with S. If it adopts the House bill, it will start with H.R.

CONFERENCE COMMITTEE

HOUSE AND SENATE VOTE

SPEAKER OF THE HOUSE AND VICE PRESIDENT SIGN BILL

The No School on Fridays bill cleared committees in the House and Senate. It passed in the House and Senate as separate versions. The bill then went to conference committee for markup by senators and representatives. The revised bill passed out of conference committee as a conference report, or single version approved by the House and Senate. The House and Senate passed the report and submitted it to the president to sign or veto.

CHAPTER 7
TO THE PRESIDENT: GETTING SIGNED INTO LAW

TRUE OR FALSE? Bills are sent to the president through the mail. False. Bills are delivered by hand.

At 9:00 A.M., Tim Schultz, a House staff person, enters the president's office in the White House. He announces to the secretary that he has a bill related to education and allowing schools to close on Fridays for the president's consideration.

(Above) All bills that make it through conference committee are delivered to the Oval Office in the White House for the president's review.

The secretary stamps the bill with the date and time it was received. The secretary will pass it on to the president.

The president has a tough decision to make. He would like to sign H.R. 1022 into law because he is a friend of Representative Smith and Senator Moe. They are from the same political party as the president, and he usually agrees with their bills. But in this case, he doesn't agree with them. He thinks that education is very important and that school should be held on Fridays. He believes kids need as much schooling as they can get.

President Bill Clinton reads a bill. The president uses information from many sources in deciding whether to sign or veto a bill.

THE FINAL SAY

The president has three choices when bills are presented to him: sign, veto, or do nothing. If the president agrees with the bill, he can sign it, and it becomes law. If he disagrees with the bill, he can veto it. The bill will not become a law unless Congress votes to override the veto. To override the veto, two-thirds of the members of both the House and the Senate have to pass the bill again.
The president has ten days to either sign or veto the bill. If the president doesn't do anything, then the bill becomes law. This is true only when Congress is in session. If Congress adjourns, or ends its session, before those ten days are up, then the bill does not become law. This is called a pocket veto.

(Right) The Buck Stops Here was President Harry S. Truman's view of his responsibilities. These included signing or vetoing bills.

The president wants to veto the bill, to stop it from becoming a law. But he needs to make sure he has all his facts straight. His staff has prepared a report listing the reasons people supported or rejected the bill when it was before Congress.

President Ulysses S. Grant writes a letter of veto, explaining his decision to Congress and the public. President Grant served from 1869 until 1877.

The president stays up until 2:00 A.M. reading through this report. Although he thinks there are good arguments from both sides, he hasn't changed his mind. He is going to veto the bill.

At 9:00 A.M. the next day, the president sits at his desk in the Oval Office. He reads over the final draft of his veto message. In part, the letter reads: "I have always believed that education is the most important gift we can give the children of this country. I do not want to do anything to interfere with education. Because of this, I am not signing this bill."

The bill, which has gone through all the steps of becoming a law, is called an act. Because the president vetoed it instead of signing it, the act did not become a law. Representative Smith and Senator Moe don't think they can get enough votes to override the president's veto. But when Congress meets again next year, Representative Smith and Senator Moe just may reintroduce their bills. The bills could go through all the steps of becoming a law again—being referred to a committee; having a hearing; being reported out of committee; being placed on a calendar; being debated on the House and Senate floors; being voted on; and finally, perhaps, making it to the president's desk again. Do you think this idea will become a law then?

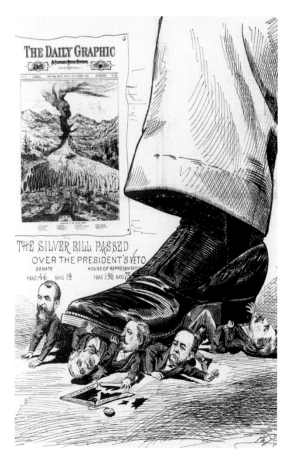

This political cartoon from a newspaper of the 1800s shows Congress "putting its foot down," or overriding a president's veto and passing a bill into law.

SIGNING A BILL

When the president signs bills into law, an official signing ceremony sometimes takes place at the White House. The president may sign many bills on one day. The bills' sponsors from the Senate and the House, as well as other people who helped get the bills passed, will gather with the president in the Rose Garden. If an important bill is going to get signed, newspaper reporters and television cameras will probably be there, too. The president uses a different pen to sign each bill. Sometimes he uses several pens. After signing the bill, he hands the pens to the bill's sponsors and to other people to whom the new law is important.

Sometimes the president does not have a ceremony but just signs bills and sends them back to Congress. Usually, the president does this with less important or less popular bills.

President George W. Bush signs a bill into law. The pens he uses for signing will go to sponsors and other supporters of the bill.

THE LIFE OF A BILL

1) IDEA

2) SUPPORT

3) INTEREST GROUP

7) THE COMMITTEE STUDIES THE BILL

8) THE BILL GOES ON A CALENDAR

9) CONSIDERATION BY THE HOUSE

13) THE BILL GOES BACK TO THE FULL SENATE

14) CONFERENCE COMMITTEE ACTION

15) THE BILL IS PRINTED

GLOSSARY

act: a bill that has been passed by both the House and the Senate and has been either signed or vetoed by the president

amendment: a change in a bill; also refers to an addition to the U.S. Constitution

bill: a draft of a law

calendar: a list of bills waiting to be decided by the House or the Senate

cloture: the only procedure through which senators can end, or close, a filibuster and force a vote on a bill. If three-fifths of the full Senate (normally sixty senators) votes for cloture, the debate must end within thirty hours. Once debate ends, senators vote on the bill.

companion bills: similar bills introduced in both the House and the Senate

conference committee: a committee made up of members from both the House and the Senate to work out differences between two versions of the same bill

drafting a bill: writing a bill in the proper language and form

filibuster: to talk for a long time in the Senate chamber to prevent a vote from taking place

floor: the part of the House or Senate chamber where members of Congress meet for official business

hearing: a committee meeting held in either the House or Senate at which members consider bills and hear arguments on both sides of an issue

interest group: a group that tries to convince senators and representatives to vote a certain way on particular bills

lobbyist: a person who works to convince members of Congress to pass, change, or defeat certain bills

pocket veto: an automatic veto that occurs when Congress adjourns (ends its session) less than ten days after the president receives a bill but before the president has signed or vetoed the bill

presiding officer: in the House, the Speaker. In the Senate, the majority leader, the president pro tempore (temporary president), or, for official occasions, the vice president of the United States

quorum: the number of members who must be present on the floor to conduct official business—51 in the Senate and 218 in the House

report out: to return a bill to the House or Senate from a committee, with recommendations either for or against the bill

rider: an unrelated amendment attached to a bill

rules: the special conditions for handling a bill on the House floor, determined by the Rules Committee

session: the yearly meeting of Congress

Speaker of the House: the leader of the House of Representatives

subcommittee: a smaller committee set up within a full committee to hold hearings on bills related to a particular topic

veto: the power of the president to stop a bill from becoming law

BIBLIOGRAPHY

Coy, Harold. *The First Book of Congress.* New York: Franklin Watts, 1965.

Coy, Harold, and Barbara L. Dammann. *Congress.* Rev. ed. New York: Franklin Watts, 1981.

Gourse, Leslie. *The Congress.* New York: Franklin Watts, 1994.

Johnson, Gerald W. *The Congress.* New York: William Morrow and Company, 1963.

National Science Teachers Association. *How a Bill Becomes a Law to Conserve Energy.* Washington, D.C.: U.S. Department of Energy, 1977.

"Welcome to Project Vote Smart." *Project Vote Smart.* 2002. <http://www.vote-smart.org/ce/congresstrack/billtolaw.phtml> (April 2003).

FURTHER READING AND WEBSITES

BOOKS

Duvall, Jill. *Congressional Committees*. New York: Franklin Watts, 1997. This book examines the different types of committees in Congress, their functions, leadership, and influences.

Feldman, Ruth Tenzer. *How Congress Works: A Look at the Legislative Branch*. Minneapolis: Lerner Publications Company, 2004. This book offers readers an easily understandable explanation of Congress's work and its role in the U.S. government.

Gourse, Leslie. *The Congress*. New York: Franklin Watts, 1994. This book provides an introduction to Congress, including discussions of the role of Congress, committee structure, and leadership positions.

Heath, David. *The Congress of the United States*. Mankato, MN: Capstone High/Low Books, 1999. This book discusses the history and structure of the two branches of Congress and how they make laws.

Jones, Veda Boyd, and Arthur Meier Schlesinger. *The Senate*. New York: Chelsea House Publishers, 2000. This book discusses the history and duties of the U.S. Senate and follows a day in the life of one of its members.

Kowalski, Kathiann M. *Order in the Court: A Look at the Judicial Branch*. Minneapolis: Lerner Publications Company, 2004. Through text, images, and diagrams, this book explains the role of the Supreme Court in the U.S. government, as well as its role in the lawmaking process and the interpretation of laws.

Landau, Elaine. *The President's Work: A Look at the Executive Branch*. Minneapolis: Lerner Publications Company, 2004. This book uses descriptive text, photographs, and illustrations to examine the roles and responsibilities of the president and the executive branch of the U.S. government.

Partner, David. *The House of Representatives*. New York: Chelsea House Publishers, 2000. This book discusses the history and duties of the U.S. House of Representatives and follows a day in the life of one of its members.

Sandak, Cass R. *Lobbying*. 1995. Reprint, New York: Twenty-First Century Books, 1997. This book helps readers understand the role that interest groups and lobbying play in making laws.

Sanders, Mark C. *Congress*. New York: Raintree Steck-Vaughn, 2001. This book provides a detailed look at how Congress works, including how bills become laws.

Ventura, Jesse, with Herón Márquez. *Jesse Ventura Tells It like It Is: America's Most Outspoken Governor Speaks Out about Government.* Minneapolis: Lerner Publications Company, 2002. Former Minnesota governor Jesse Ventura expresses his views on politics and government and the importance of citizen involvement to make them work.

WEBSITES

Congress for Kids
<http://www.congressforkids.net/>
This website offers an online tour of the federal government for kids, including many fun activities relating to Congress. It is part of the Dirksen Congressional Center, a nonprofit group that does not support any one political party.

Project Vote Smart
<http://www.vote-smart.org/ce/congresstrack/billtolaw.phtml>
This website provides a very detailed outline of how a bill becomes a law and also has a glossary of many political terms. It is part of Project Vote Smart, a nonprofit group that provides the public with information about elected officials and candidates for political office. Project Vote Smart does not support any one political party.

Talk to Gov.Com
<http://www.talktogov.com/howabill.htm>
This website has a step-by-step guide to how a bill becomes a law. It is part of TalkToGov, a nonprofit group aimed at helping people understand government. TalkToGov does not support any one political party.

CONTACTS FOR STUDENTS

The following groups can be contacted to learn more about getting involved in some favorite causes and learning more about political parties and how they work. Many more sites can be found on the Internet. If you have an idea that you'd like to become a law, here are some places to get started.

Common Cause
<http://www.commoncause.org>
A nonpartisan organization that works for open, accountable government and the right of all citizens to be involved in our nation's public policies

Congress.org: Write to Congress and the President
<http://www.congress.org/congressorg/home>
This site offers contact links to the president and federal and state congresspeople.

Democracy Matters
<http://www.democracymatters.org>
Informs and engages students and communities to strengthen our democracy

Democratic National Committee
<http://www.democrats.org>
The national office for the Democratic Party

Girls' Pipeline to Power
<http://www.girlspipeline.org/pipeline.shtml>
Helps girls become school and community activists and provides leadership opportunities; founded by the Patriots' Trail Girl Scout Council

National Education Association
<http://www.nea.org>
The nation's leading organization committed to the advancement of public education

Republican National Committee
<http://www.rnc.org>
The national office for the Republican Party

Sierra Club
<http://www.sierraclub.org>
The country's oldest and largest grassroots environmental organization works to protect our communities and the planet

United States Student Association
<http://www.usstudents.org>
This website gives students a way to communicate directly with Congress, the White House, and the Department of Education. If you have any questions or would like to post something up on their calendar, e-mail the association at <comm@usstudents.org>.

INDEX

ABOUT THE AUTHOR

Sandy Donovan has written many books for young readers, on topics including history, civics, and biology. Donovan has also worked as a newspaper reporter and a magazine editor, and she holds a bachelor's degree in journalism and a master's degree in public policy. She has lived and traveled in Europe, Asia, and the Middle East. She lives in Minneapolis, Minnesota, with her husband and son. Donovan's other titles include *Protecting America: A Look at the People Who Keep Our Country Safe, Running for Office: A Look at Political Campaigns,* and *The Channel Tunnel.*

PHOTO ACKNOWLEDGMENTS

The photographs and illustrations in this book are reproduced with the permission of: © Joseph Sohm/ChromoSohm Inc./CORBIS, p. 4; Lyndon B. Johnson Library, p. 5; © KRAFT BROOKS/CORBIS SYGMA, p. 6; © Graham Douglas/CORBIS SYGMA, p. 7; © Szenes Jason/CORBIS SYGMA, p. 8; © LOPRESSE/CORBIS SYGMA, p. 9; © Catherine Karnow/CORBIS, p. 10; © CORBIS, pp. 11, 31, 43, 44; © Todd Strand/Independent Picture Service, p. 13 (left); Library of Congress, pp. 13 (right), 15; courtesy of the office of Representative George Miller, p. 14 (bottom left); courtesy of the office of Senator Christopher Dodd, p. 14 (top right); courtesy of the United States Printing Office, pp. 14 (top left, bottom right), 24, 25, 38; Bill Hauser, pp. 16, 22, 39, 46–47; © Reuters NewMedia Inc./CORBIS, pp. 17, 20, 35; © Bettmann/CORBIS, pp. 19, 29, 32, 33, 37; © AFP/CORBIS, pp. 21, 45; © Sandy Felsenthal/CORBIS, p. 23; © Hulton|Archive, p. 27; © The *New Yorker* Collection 1995 Michael Crawford from cartoonbank.com. All rights reserved, p. 28; © Wally McNamee/CORBIS, p. 40; © MARKOWITZ JEFFREY/CORBIS SYGMA, p. 41; courtesy of the Harry S. Truman Library, p. 42.

ML   10/03